Dividend Investing:

Concise & 2nd Edition

Tony Pow

Why you want to read this book

It should improve your financial health substantially.

- This book has over 60 pages (6*9) and is about double the size of its competitors with similar price range.

- A best seller was written by a young writer whose main income was from his books and none from his investing. Most of my income is from investing.

- Many popular books claiming the authors making millions. However, usually their techniques are hard to follow. Many admitted they had been bankrupted many times. My techniques minimize risking our money. Paper test your technique first.

- There are many popular books combining technical and some fundamentals. They worked very well at one time and folks making millions following the advices. However, look at their recent performances of the last five years.

- One book describes ROE as the only theme (with the story of the life of the author to fill up the book).

My motivation to write this book

I would like to share my experiences, both good and bad. I use simple-to-follow techniques using the free (or low-cost) resources available to us.

Click the link for the articles I wrote for SeekingAlpha.com, a site for investors. http://seekingalpha.com/author/tony-pow/articles

Contents

Why you want to read this book 2

Why you invest 4

Introduction...5

Dividend investing 10

   1   The basics 11

   2   More on dividend stocks 14

   3   Potential problems 16

   4   Dividend growth 18

   5   Are dividend stocks better? 19

Section I: Dividends Screening 23

   1   Screening dividend stocks with Finviz.............................24

Section II: Pick stocks for appreciation 27

   1   Simplest way to evaluate stocks 28

   2   Finviz parameters 31

   3   Intangibles 38

   4   Qualitative analysis...42

   5   *When to sell a stock* 46

   6   Sectors to be cautious with 51

Section III: Market timing..54

   1   Simplest market timing...55

Appendix 1 – All my books...56

   Best stocks to buy for 2022 (avail. after Dec. 15, 21)..................57

Appendix 2 – Complete the Art of Investing 58

   Sector Rotation: 21 Strategies 62

Appendix 3 - Our window to the investing world 63

Appendix 4 - ETFs / Mutual Funds 64

Why you invest

You need to learn about investing sooner or later in your life. You need to take some calculated risks.

Compare the returns of the following assets: cash, CDs, treasury bills, bonds, real estate and stocks. We start with the risk-free investments and end with the riskiest. It turns out that the average returns are in the opposite order. Cash and CDs are not risk-free as inflation eats our profits. For example, the real return is negative for the 2% return in a CD and a 3% inflation rate. In addition you have to pay taxes for the 'returns'. Our capitalist system punishes us for not taking risk.

There are two kinds of risk: blind risk and calculated risk. If you buy a stock due to a recommendation from a commentator on TV or a tip, most likely you are taking a blind risk. It would be the same in buying a house without thoroughly evaluating the house and its neighborhood. When you buy stocks with a proven strategy (i.e. when/what stocks to buy and when/what stocks to sell), you are taking a calculated risk. In the long run, stocks with calculated and educated risks are profitable.

Be a turtle investor by investing in value stocks and holding for longer time periods (a year or more). "Buy and Monitor" is better an approach than "Buy and Hold" as some could lose all the stock values such as in the failure of Enron.

For experienced investors, shorting, short-term trading and covered calls would make you good profits. Simple market timing would reduce your losses during market down turns. If you buy a market ETF and use my simple market timing, you should have beaten the market by a wide margin from 2000 to 2019.

With so many frauds and poor management, do not trust anyone with your investing. Do not buy investing instruments that are highly marketed such as annuity and term insurance.

If you are a handy man and do not mind to satisfy the constant requests of your tenants, buy real estate in growing areas could be very profitable in the long run. Take advantage of the tax laws such as investing in a 401K especially the part that is matched by your company and/or a Roth IRA.

Introduction

This strategy is expected to be popular for the next 10 years or until the average CD rate beats the average dividend rate. We have a lot of retirees who depend on income from investments. The low interest rates from CDs and bonds drive these folks to dividend stocks.

Here is a simple screen to find these stocks. First find the stocks that have dividend rates more than 2% (about half of all S&P 500 stocks). Take out those sectors that give dividends as a return of equity (REITs and many partnerships). Eliminate the stocks with bad fundamentals such as high expected P/E (and earnings is negative), high debt (compared to companies in the same sector), etc. Next ensure that they have a good history of maintaining or increasing dividends (i.e. dividend growth).

As of 5-2014, it has been working well for the last five years. Be cautious on bank stocks, the drug companies, the miners and the insurers. I ignore foreign companies and ADRs (those foreign companies listed in the U.S. exchange). I prefer larger companies.

However, when a strategy is over-used, it may not work any longer. There may be a mild bubble on these dividend stocks due to too many followers. We will discuss how to protect our dividend portfolios.

In addition, we should not buy (actually should sell most stocks you own) stocks during a market plunge. Since 2000, we have two market plunges with an average loss of over 45%. We hope to have a maximum loss of 25% instead of 45%; most techniques depend on price movements and hence we cannot detect the peaks and bottoms. There are at least three variations on dividends:

1. Dividends given to stock owners (registered on and before the **ex-div date**).
2. Covered Calls. You can receive dividends while 'renting' your stocks.
3. DRIPs, Dividend Reinvest Plan.
http://en.wikipedia.org/wiki/Dividend_reinvestment_plan

This book started with Market Timing. When the market is going to plunge, most stocks including dividend stocks will lose values. Hence, do not buy any stocks and even sell most stocks when you receive the exit signal.

I have a simple chart to identify market plunges. It depends on the stock data, so it will not identify the peaks and the bottoms precisely, but it will spare you for further losses and will instruct you when to reenter the market. It worked for the last two market crashes. It will detect the next crash, and hopefully it will give us enough time to react as the last two.

The selected web site identifies stocks with good dividends. Ignore those purchases that do not meet our initial requirements. We should have identified a few stocks for further evaluation.

I use fundamental metrics to ensure they are fundamentally sound. Many fundamental analyses are available free from many sites. Then look for intangibles and do a thorough qualitative analysis on each selected stock. There is no magic formula, but due diligence will pay off in the long run. This book does not promise overnight wealth.

Other topics include how to set order prices, stop loss, tax considerations and a trade plan. When to sell a stock is important. Technical analysis is used sparingly but it could be very useful.

Periodically review your big losers and big gainers to see whether any lessons to be learned.

As in any strategy, you need to start with paper testing and then with limited positions. There are many pitfalls in following insider purchases. It is safer to buy stocks with good fundamentals and protect the losses with stops.

This book is intended for a retail investor and I am one myself. This book is not written by a journalist or a professional writer who may never make a buck in the stock market. This book is part of the Concise Series. They include one or few most important chapters from my full-size books. Ignore some of the references to chapters in the full-size book. It competes with books with similar size and price.

How this book is organized

This book has 3 sections covering most areas in dividend trading.

Most graphs are in landscape orientation for both paperback and e-readers. Some graphs may not be displayed adequately on a small screen of an e-reader. E-readers may be available in the current version of Windows, so you can read e-books on the larger screen of your PC. For better orientation, just flip the e-readers 90 degrees.

A link is usually included for these screens. Copy it to your browser to display the graphs on your PC if desirable. Instructions on how to produce some graphs are provided as you should try them out. One example is how to produce a chart on detecting market crashes.

It is easier to display some tables in landscape mode, which can be selected in your e-reader. Select a table or a graph via your e-reader to display it to fit the screen.

The font size and page size of most e-book formats can be adjusted. The unknown, special character is the "smiling face" that the current Kindle does not convert correctly as of this writing.

There are clickable links to web articles. Most of them are from my own web sites and public web sites such as Wikipedia. Some public links may not be available in the future as they are not under my control.

Fidelity Video provides video clips to explain some basic terms and it may require Fidelity customers to sign on in order to view them. Check the trial offer from Fidelity. YouTube offers similar video lessons.

These links extend the usefulness of this book by making available specific topics that may not be interesting to every reader.

The current version provides most of the links the paperback readers can enter into your browser. Get the same information by entering a search in Wikipedia such as Dogs of Dow.

Investopedia is another source beside Wikipedia.
http://www.investopedia.com/

'Afterthoughts' includes my additional comments and comments from others. Readers can make comments in this book's website. These comments may be included in the Afterthoughts in subsequent revisions, with the commenter's last name redacted. It is the section of the article for freer and informal discussion.

There are fillers with tips and jokes to fill up the empty space of the printed book.

For convenience, this book uses SPY, an Exchange Traded Fund (ETF) simulating the S&P 500, as the benchmark for the market.

Annualized returns (Return * 365 / (Days between)) are used where appropriate for more meaningful comparison. To illustrate, I have a 10% return in 6 months, a 10% in a year and a 10% in 2 years. It is more meaningful to use annualized returns of 20%, 10% and 5% respectively for the 6-month return, the one-year return and the 2-year return in this example.

Usually I do not include the dividend, so you can add an estimated 1.5% to the annualized return. In addition, compound interest is not used for easier calculation, so the actual return could be even better.

About the author
I graduated from Cal. State University at San Jose in Industrial Engineering and University of Mass. in Amherst with a MS in Industrial Engineering. I have been an investor for over 30 years.

Dedication
To all retail investors and future retail investors including my grandchildren. I sincerely hope this book will build bridges with fellow investors with different backgrounds.

Acknowledgement
Thanks to Seeking Alpha, Wikipedia and Investopedia for the many helpful links to enrich this book. Yahoo!Finance and Finviz.com for the tools and charts used in this book.

Important notices
© 2014-22 Tony Pow. Email ID: pow_tony@yahoo.com

Version	Paperback	eBooks
1.0	05/14	05/14
2.0	08/16	08/16
3.0	10/19	10/19
4.0	02/20	02/20
4.3	11/21	11/21

Printed version of ISBN-13: 978-1499381719 or ISBN-10: 1499381719
No part of this book can be reproduced in any form without the written approval of the author. Book store managers can order this book from Createspace.com.
Book update.
https://ebmyth.blogspot.com/2020/12/updates-for-all-books.html

Disclaimer

Do not gamble money that you cannot afford to lose. Past performance is a guideline and does not guarantee future performance.

All information is believed to be accurate, but there it is not guaranteed. All the strategies described have no guarantee that they will make money and they may lose money. Do not trade without doing due diligence and be warned that most data would be obsolete. All my articles and the associated data are for informational purposes only. I'm not a professional investment counselor or a tax professional. Seek one before you make any investment decision.

The above mentioned also applies for all other advice such as on accounting, taxes, health and any topic mentioned in this book. I am not a professional in any of these fields. Same for all the links contained in this book. Some articles may offend some one or some organization unintentionally. If I did, I'm sorry about that. I am politically and religiously neutral. I try my best effort to ensure the accuracy of my articles. Data also from different sources was believed to be accurate. However, there is no guarantee that they are accurate and suitable for the current market conditions and /or your individual situations. I and my publisher are not liable for any damages in using this book.

What is DRIP

DRIP stands for dividend reinvestment plan. It uses the dividend to buy more stock of the company that pays the dividend automatically and most likely with no commission and sometimes at 2-3% discount.

I participated in these plans before. After a long while, the stocks bought from dividends worth more than the initial stocks. Need to keep track of the cost basis of the bought stocks when you sell these stocks.

Check out whether the company and/or your broker offer such program. There are many sites to have more info of DRIPs such as Money Paper. Google 'DRIP'.

https://www.directinvesting.com/

Dividend investing

This strategy is expected to be popular for the next 10 years or until the average CD rate beats the average dividend rate. We have a lot of retirees who depend on income from investments. The low interest rates from CDs and bonds drive these folks to dividend stocks.

Here is a simple screen to find these stocks. First find the stocks that have dividend rates more than 2% (about half of all S&P 500 stocks). Take out those sectors that give dividends as a return of equity (REITs and many partnerships). Eliminate the stocks with bad fundamentals such as high expected P/E (and earnings is negative), high debt (compared to companies in the same sector), etc. Next ensure that they have a good history of maintaining or increasing dividends (i.e. dividend growth).

As of 5-2014, it has been working well for the last five years. Be cautious on bank stocks, the drug companies, the miners and the insurers. I ignore foreign companies and ADRs (those foreign companies listed in the U.S. exchange). I prefer larger companies.

However, when a strategy is overused, it may not work any longer. There may be a mild bubble on these dividend stocks due to too many followers. We will discuss how to protect our dividend portfolios.

In addition, we should not buy (actually should sell most stocks you own) stocks during a market plunge. Since 2000, we have had two market plunges with an average loss of over 45%. We hope to have a maximum loss of 25% instead of 45%; most techniques depend on price movements and hence we cannot detect the peaks and bottoms. There are at least three variations on dividends:

4. Dividends given to stock owners (registered on and before the **ex-div date**).
5. Covered Calls. You can receive dividends while 'renting' your stocks.
6. DRIPs, Dividend Reinvest Plan.
   http://en.wikipedia.org/wiki/Dividend_reinvestment_plan

1   The basics

Basic ratios for dividend stocks

- **Ex-dividend date**

You will be eligible for dividends if you have your stock on the record. You want to buy the stock earlier, or on ex-dividend date in order to receive the dividend.

- Payout Ratio

It is the dividend / profit. Too high a ratio may not be good as the company does not plow back the profit into research / development. Most mature companies have higher payout ratios as they do not need to plow back into research / development compared to high-tech companies.

The other option of using the company's cash is in a stock buyback that would increase the stock values in theory.

Earnings per share = Earnings / Outstanding Shares.

When 'Earnings' is fixed but Outstanding Shares are reduced, the ratio looks good deceptively. The management does this often as it would boost the values of their options.

- Dividend Yield.

It is equal to Dividend / Price.

Why companies pay dividends

Companies can use the profit by plowing back cash into research / development, buying back its stocks, acquiring companies and/or giving dividends to the stockholders. In theory, the company should consider the option most beneficial to the average stockholder. In practice, the management tries to benefit themselves by choosing the option best to appreciate their stocks and hence the stock options they own.

My additions to conventional dividend investing

Hopefully my additions would improve the performance of this strategy.

- I add market timing to dividend investing. You need to sell most stocks before a market plunge and buy them back as indicated by the market timing indicator.

- Diversify your portfolio. Keep 10 stocks for a portfolio of less than a million dollars. Ensure no more than 3 stocks are in the same sector. Keep 20 stocks for a portfolio over a million dollars. Holding too many stocks would require more of your time that would be better spent in evaluating individual stocks. Holding too few stocks would impact your portfolio when one stock has a big loss.

   It is just my recommendation. Vary your holding size, your portfolio size and your knowledge in investing.

- Stick with stocks with a stock price over $2, an average daily volume of over 10,000 shares (8,000 for stock prices over $20) and a market cap over 200 million.

   Most big winners usually are in the price range of between $2 and $15 price and a market cap of between 200 million and 800 million. They represent the stocks that institutional investors are ignoring due to their restrictions. This is just a general guideline. Change them according to your requirements.

   I prefer to skip stocks of most emerging countries, especially the smaller companies as I do not trust their financial statements.

- Ignore the subscription services or books claiming that they make over 30% consistently. Some even have examples of making 5,000%. Most likely they tell you about the winners but not their losers.

   Check whether their portfolio uses cash or not. Most likely those portfolios that consistently make over 30% are not real.

   Alternatively they have 10 portfolios and they may only show you the one that makes a good profit. They could use the most favorable trades for the day for their virtual account. For example, the stock rose 20% late in the day and they claimed that they bought it on the open hour.

   When they back test their strategies, they can cheat on their performances with survivor bias (i.e. those bankrupted stocks are not in the historical database). If their returns are that great, do you think they really want to share their secrets with a stranger like you?

Some made a big fortune and lost it all. So, the turtle investors who make small profits consistently win. Market timing and diversifying our portfolios help us win consistently in the long run.

Besides screening dividend stocks yourself, there are many sites providing this information. You can google 'dividend stocks'. The following are some of them.

TopYields
http://www.topyields.nl/Top-dividend-yields-of-Dividend-Aristocrats.php

An ETF on Dividend Aristocrats
http://etfdb.com/index/sp-high-yield-dividend-aristocrats-index/

From Wikipedia on S&P Dividend Aristocrats
http://en.wikipedia.org/wiki/THE S&P_500_Dividend_Aristocrats

There are many sites to screen dividend stocks. I select Finviz.com as that should give us good results most of the time and it is free. In addition, we use the same site for market timing using SMA-20% and SMA-50%.

Screening is only the first step. You need to filter out the good stocks from the bad ones. When you have a handful of stocks, evaluate each one.

Links Building a portfolio: https://www.youtube.com/watch?v=ryN1aQxSefQ

Best dividend ETF: https://www.youtube.com/watch?v=TPSw7On2gUo
https://www.youtube.com/watch?v=YBCmJU8osOo

Filler.
DRIP stands for dividend reinvestment plan. It uses the dividend to buy more stock of the company that pays the dividend automatically, and most likely with no commissions and some gives discounts of 2-3%.

I have participated in these plans before. After a long while, the stocks bought from dividends were worth more than the initial stock prices. You need to keep track of the cost basis of the purchased stocks when you sell these stocks. Check out whether the company and/or your broker offer such programs. There are many sites that have more info of DRIPs such as Money Paper https://www.directinvesting.com/.

2 More on dividend stocks

- Check out the tax rate for dividends and the tax rate for your tax bracket with a qualified professional and act accordingly.

- It makes sense to evaluate more carefully the stocks with the top 25 dividend yield stocks. If the yield is that good, they could have some problems. It also could be yesterday's darlings. Try the next 25 according to an article I read. You need to further analyze each stock especially on the fundamentals. Ensure the high-dividend yields are not due to the return of capital as in some REITs and partnerships; it could be the reason why the top 25 dividend yield stocks do not perform.

- Use CCC charts by David Fish.
  http://dripinvesting.org/tools/tools.asp

- A good article on dividend stocks.
  (http://seekingalpha.com/article/1591272-the-7-habits-of-highly-effective-dividend-growth-investors?source=kizur)

- Check their payout ratios. When the company plows back most of its profit to dividends, the company will not grow as much. Many mature companies are fine in doing this. I prefer a payout ratio between 50-70%.

- Be careful in the last quarter such as in 2012 in identifying dividend and dividend growth stocks. It is a period when companies pay extra dividends expecting higher tax rates for their stockholders next year.

  REITs must pay out 90% of their earnings to maintain their REIT status. Their dividends are taxed as ordinary income.

- Buffett on dividends.
  (http://kinderflow.blogspot.com/2013/08/dividends-warren-buffett.html)

- Buy the companies that have a lot of cash and pay little or no dividends. There is a good chance these companies will pay dividends, or increase their dividends and the stock prices would usually appreciate.

- As of 7/2013, corporations had a lot of cash with low debt comparatively. Coupled with low interest rates and a weak economy, corporations increase their dividends and buy back their own stocks.

- Here is a site to grade dividend stocks.
  http://navelliergrowth.investorplace.com/dividend-grader/

- A successful story on dividend investing.
  http://finance.yahoo.com/news/heres-janitor-amassed-8m-fortune-234459317.html

- Here is another set of criteria for dividend stocks.

  - Dividend yield over 2.5% (or at least .5% above the average of dividend yield of all the S&P 500 stocks).
  - Dividend growth for the last 5 years is zero or higher.
  - Profit growth is positive for the last 5 years.
  - Dividend payout is under 70%.
  - P/E under 25 and earnings are positive.
  - ROE is over 8%.

  If you do not find too many of these stocks, the dividend stocks may be overbought.

- There are many other sources for income besides dividends:
  - You can sell some shares. Be sure to check out the tax consequences.
  - Buy bonds. Long-term bonds are favorable when the interest rates are high. Check the S&P bond rating. Forget the bonds rated BBB and below.
  - REITs and energy royalty trusts. Many require you to file extra forms if they are in taxable accounts.

Links

Building a portfolio: https://www.youtube.com/watch?v=ryN1aQxSefQ

https://www.youtube.com/watch?v=q3IG95iWwTU

3   Potential problems

When a strategy is overused, it creates a bubble. The only exception is the gold rush in 2010 due to printing too much money and gold had been down for a long time. When the shoe shine boy told a famous Wall Street investor he was buying stocks that smart investors unloaded everything. He knew the boy did not do any research and it was the herd mentality.

When Sarah Cohen told the TV reporter she was into dividend stocks, she seemed to be the shoe shine boy except she was prettier and she had a lot of skills but not in investing.

When the massive money flows into ETFs specialized in dividend stocks, it is a mild bubble. History tells us that the average retail investor always selects the wrong side of the market. So far, Fidelity's money fund flow has been a good contrary indicator for the market.

Past performance does not guarantee future performance unless the market conditions are the same, but it seldom happens. There are many examples such as the 2000's internet bust. Investing in dividend stocks today (2015) is still a mild bubble by many standards. Dividend stocks perform better than the market but not by a large amount. When the financial companies such as Lehman Brothers, AIG and Bear Sterns are included, dividend stocks do not perform that well.

Today there are several articles on how dividend stocks are overvalued. The premium on dividend stocks has been the highest in the last 30 years.

Consider Total Return

Total Return = Appreciation + Dividend + Covered Call (if used) - Taxes – Inflation

The institutional investors drive the market. They consider their total return. Appreciation is usually more favorable than dividend for most of their wealthy investors tax-wise in most cases.

You do not have to realize the gains (for tax purposes) on capital gains in taxable accounts. When you die, the cost basis will be stepped up. In a

word, you have more control with capital gains but not with dividends. Check the current low-tax laws.
(http://en.wikipedia.org/wiki/Dividend_tax#United_States).

Afterthoughts

- Check the dividend performances and switch when they do not perform.
  http://seekingalpha.com/data/dividends
- Myths.
  http://money.usnews.com/money/blogs/the-smarter-mutual-fund-investor/2014/02/04/7-myths-about-dividend-paying-stocks
- SA article in 2016.
  http://seekingalpha.com/article/3901726-fate-49-dividend-aristocrats-early-1990s-may-give-nightmares

Filler

I got a call from Buffett asking me to lead their stock research.
I asked him why for nobody such as myself. No kidding.

He told me that he should have read my book Scoring Stocks to buy Apple instead of IBM in May, 2013. It would save his company millions of dollars minus $10 for my book. Not to mention the market timing technique that had worked in the last two major market plunges.

I told him, "OK, I'll beat your mediocre returns of the last 5 years."
He said, "You can do better than that and at least beat SPY. If you do so, no one will be that stupid to leave my fund and pay the hefty capital gain taxes."

I told him, "I cannot beat the market as you are the market especially after your expensive fees. In addition, I do not know how to avoid day traders from riding my wagon in trading. Also most of my big profits were made in small stocks that your fund cannot trade besides owning the company."

I woke up trembling. I'm glad it is only a nightmare.

4   Dividend growth

This strategy seemed to be working fine for a long time. It is partly due to the low interest rates. Retirees cannot depend on the bonds for income, so they switch to stocks that pay good dividends.

In 2015, we have to pay a premium for stocks paying high dividends. When will it end? You can examine the performance of any ETF such as DVY that specializes on high-dividend stocks for the last month and the previous three months. When they performed worse than SPY (an ETF simulating the S&P 500 stocks), most likely this mild bubble would burst soon. On 9/2015, they are not doing well as a group.

A list of dividend ETFs. http://www.dividend.com/dividend-etfs/

Filler

Quantitative Easing is supposed to stimulate the economy, create jobs and increase inflation. As of 3-2015, it has not for most countries including the U.S.

The money has not been passed to the small businesses that generate the most jobs; we should let the SBA assign the loans. Large businesses use most of the cheap money to generate products / services to increase supply and hence deflation is the norm. Stock buybacks do not generate the value as illustrated by my PE (modified from the current P/E).

My PE = (Price − Cash + Debt) / Expected Earnings
        all expressed in per share

It is better but more work to use "Net Current Asset" instead of Cash.

The big banks lend money to investors and that explains why the stock market is booming and we have record-high margin debt. It also widens the wealth gap generating inequality conflicts.

5 Are dividend stocks better?

There are continuous debates for and against dividend stocks / dividend growth stocks. I hope this article will settle the debates. If you're making money with any strategy recently, stick with it. From my test, I conclude that dividend stocks / dividend growth stocks are worse off than non-dividend stocks. Please read it with an open mind if you are a dividend lover.

Do not be biased and data fit to back up your conclusions. Ensure the test can be reproduced with identical results, and there is no cherry picking and no bias. Ensure the number of stocks and the number of tests are large enough so the results are statistically acceptable.

Here is my test procedure. It would be a sample test procedure that can be deplored for other strategies.

A test consists of selecting a number of stocks according to a specific criterion such as the 30 stocks giving top dividends. The performance of the test is defined as the average return of the specific number of stocks (30 in my test) after a period of time (a year in my test).

- I have four tests: Dividend Stocks, Dividend Growth Stocks, Non-Dividend Stocks and All Stocks. Select the top 30 stocks for each test.
- There are 10 tests for each month within each test. The first test starts at the beginning of the year and will end at the end of the year. The results of the 10 tests are averaged.
- The last ten years resemble the current market better than older dates do.
- The start date was Jan. 2 as Jan. 1 is a holiday. In some tests, it is Jan. 3 or Jan. 4 due to weekends.
- The results are annualized (= Return * 365 /No. of days tested).
- The database is S&P 500. Typically they are the stocks of the largest companies. 'All Stocks' consists of all stocks in the S&P 500 and it is supposed to be 500.
- Using educated estimates, I add 2% dividend yield to the performance of the S&P 500 index, 5% to dividend stocks and 4% to dividend growth stocks.
  Testing other strategies, dividends may not be as important as these tests. Alternatively, I could use ^SP500TR from Yahoo!Finance. I calculated and tested estimates. It would be very time consuming and

impossible not to use estimates as the dividend yield changes every trade session.

- Dividend growth stocks have the top dividend yields and dividend growth rates equal to or greater than 10%.
- Non-dividend stocks are stocks without dividends. Just select 30 of the non-dividend stocks in the index randomly.
- You can find performance reports on dividend ETFs or funds that specialize in dividend stocks, dividend growth stocks or a combination. Compare the results to SPY. Use them to confirm or challenge my test results.

My test has a new set of 30 stocks every year, so an exceedingly good or bad year only affects one test, not all ten tests with the exception of some stocks moving up or down for many years.

I call it the window of testing as opposed to what most funds advertise by setting $10,000 or so and letting it rise and fall for a long period (say 10 years).

- Be careful on tests using small stocks that tend to bankrupt more often. We have several large companies bankrupt and most paid good dividends. Survivor bias would give them better results than the actual results.

Result

The above tests can be reproduced from a historical database. I prefer to use a database that does not take out the delisted stocks. The result is for educational purposes only. I am not responsible for any errors.

	Avg. One-Year Return	Beat All Stocks by
Dividend	10%	-1%
Dividend Growth	9%	-12%
No Dividend	16%	62%
All Stocks	10%	N/A

- From the above table, both dividend stocks and dividend growth stocks do not beat All Stocks in this database.
- Non-dividend stocks beat All Stocks in this database by a sizable margin. They represent the companies plowing back their profits into development/research and/or buyback instead of giving dividends. I was surprised by the huge return.

- You should change your tests according to what you normally do to reflect new trading. For example, you may select 3 stocks only instead of 30 and/or delete foreign countries. However, it would be cherry picking.
- If your dividend strategy has a better return than the SPY, do not change your strategy. My tests here are simple without many other filters. Most likely you can improve your returns with better ROE, low Price /Cash Flow and low Debt/Equity.
- An article (3/1/16) from MarketWatch indicated a different finding than mine; I checked it out and DVY (a dividend ETF) did not perform that well.

Improve the test if more time is available
- Use 12 months instead of one month for each test. Hence you should have 120 tests less 11 tests due to not enough data for the last year (as of 2/15/2016).
- Take out the top performer and the bottom performer in the 30 selected stocks as judging in some sports.
- More weight in the last five years than the previous five years.

Survivor bias
My historical database does not handle the delisted stocks. When I see that there are less than 500 stocks in the database for the S&P 500, I know they just deleted the stocks taken out from the &P 500 that year. However, later on it includes new stocks added to the S&P 500 index. The adverse impact of bankrupt stocks is far higher than the acquired / merged stocks. For example, the return of the test not including Lehman Brothers makes it look far better. All the tests here look better than they actually are.

The bias can be reduced or even eliminated by:
- Larger companies as in this test. Small companies tend to go bankrupt more often.
- I use "All Stocks", which consists of all the S&P 500 stocks.
- The dividend stocks should have less survivor bias than non-dividend stocks. I did not compensate for this in my test results.
- Actually resolve the bias by including the delisted stocks if your database does not do this. You need to keep track of the delisted stocks.

A simple test

Compare DVY, a dividend ETF to SPY. Add 3% to DVY and 2% to SPY to include the estimated dividends. From the following table, 2015 was bad for dividend stocks but the performance for the last five years is about the same as SPY.

	Avg. Ann. DVY	SPY
2015	-2%	1%
1/2011-12/31/15	13%	14%

#Fillers: I wish I have a time machine

After collecting bottles for money, an old lady ordered a bowl of plain rice and ate by herself. I wish I could have ordered a meat dish for her and I was 'ashamed' of being generous.

A well-dressed gentleman offered his just-bought hamburger to a beggar. The beggar refused and asked for money instead – most likely he needed the money to buy liquor. A tale of two citizens.

During a lunch with my fellow tourists, a beautiful girl danced for our entertainment. I did not offer her anything and it had been bothering me for years.

During college, my housemates asked me to apply for food stamps. I had used only a few stamps then as I did not cook. I feel ashamed as this is my only time to collect social welfare.

We have regrets in life and we can only bring them to our graves.

#Filler:
Teach the able welfare recipients how to fish instead of giving them fish for the rest of their lives. They will not work if you take out their welfare benefits for working.

Filler: Definitions of 'ism'
Capitalism is: You do not work, you die.
Communism is: Everyone is paid the same, so there is no incentive to work harder.
Socialism: As Margaret said, when we have nothing more to give, we all go hungry like the USA is going to.

Idealism: There is no such word in reality. It only exists in our dreams. However, many treat this as it is a reality as they're still dreaming.
Feudalism. Like the Tibetan monks in the 50s. Only the monks can learn and the rest are slaves.

Section I: Dividends Screening

Besides screening dividend stocks yourself, there are many sites providing this information. You can google 'dividend stocks'. The following are some of them.

TopYields
http://www.topyields.nl/Top-dividend-yields-of-Dividend-Aristocrats.php

An ETF on Dividend Aristocrats
http://etfdb.com/index/sp-high-yield-dividend-aristocrats-index/

From Wikipedia on S&P Dividend Aristocrats
http://en.wikipedia.org/wiki/S&P_500_Dividend_Aristocrats

There are many sites to screen dividend stocks. I select finviz.com that should give us the best result and are free. In addition, we use the same site for market timing.

Screening is only the first step. Need to filter the good ones from the bad ones.

Tip

A sample trade plan

Time	Do
Tuesday	Review what stocks to buy.
Every month	Review which stocks to sell.
Every quarter	Check performance.
April	Check what to sell (if you use Sell in May)
October	Check what to buy (if you use the above strategy).
December	Trade Dogs of Dow if you use this strategy.

---

1   Screening dividend stocks with Finviz

You can use your screen from your broker or any site and then evaluate stocks using technical indicators (simpler than it looks).

Finviz.com provides a screening incorporating both fundamentals and technical metrics and it is one of the best free sites. Bring up finviz.com in your browser and select screener. You have 4 tabs: Descriptive, Fundamental, Technical and All.

Besides incorporating technical indicators, it has the following features:

- The criteria specified can be saved.

- The searched stocks can be saved in a portfolio (for paper test and performance monitor).

- For extra fee, you can have historical database (I have not tested this feature to comment).

- Some advanced technical indicators such as Candlestick (very useful as a momentum indicator).

However, it lacks the following features:

- Stocks with prices trending up in the last several weeks (such as increasing X% in previous week and y% in week before the previous week, etc.).

- Using exponential moving averages that have better predictive power than simple moving averages for momentum investing.

- Selecting ranges (for example, it cannot select all three major exchanges, market cap ranges, etc.).

Screen Criteria

The screen parameters (i.e. selection criteria) are briefly described here. They are guidelines. Adjust them to fit your risk tolerance and requirements. Monitor them from time to time as the market always changes. If you have too many stocks, restrict your criteria. If you have too few stocks, relax them.

	Metric	
Descriptive	Market Cap	+Mid (>2B)
	Avg. volume	>100K
	Analyst Rec	Buy or better
	Country	USA
	Price	>$5
	Dividend Yield	>3%
	Float Short	<10%
Fundamental	Earning	>0
	P/E	<30
	Forward P/E	<30
	Return on Equity	>15%
	Payout Ratio	>30% & <70%
	P/S	<10
Technical	200 – SMA	Price above
	RSI(14)	Not Overbought

As of 5/6/2014, I found 12 stocks that satisfy the above criteria.

In addition, they should be in one of the 3 major exchanges: NYEX, NASDQA and AMEX – finviz.com allows you to select one exchange at one time.

Finviz.com does not indicate dividend growth. Prefer positive dividend growth for the last 3 years.

Click P/E to sort with the lowest P/E first but avoid stocks with negative earnings (from P/E). If you prefer dividend over P/E, select the stocks with high dividends.

The next step is to evaluate fundamental sound stocks in next section.

I recommend to paper test your strategy using different selection criteria. When you are comfortable, commit a small sum and increase your portfolio size gradually.

Here are three articles on using Finviz.com's screener.

Investopedia.
http://www.investopedia.com/university/features-of-finviz-elite/other-chart-features.asp

How to scan using finviz (YouTube).
https://www.youtube.com/watch?v=aQ_0FTg9Cfw

Screening using technical indicators.
https://www.youtube.com/watch?v=RZRP2NeSX0s

Dividend stocks

The list changes almost every quarter as their fundamentals, the market and the sector change. Most are mature companies that do not have to plow back money for research and development. The following is a random list:

AAPL, ALV, CLX, XOM, HP, JPM, KMB, MAT, MCD, PEP, PM, WMT and WFC. In addition, you can buy an ETF (DVY) with high dividend yields or a mutual fund (FRDPX).

Section II: Pick stocks for appreciation

After the market is not risky (Section I) and we have picked up stocks (Section II), we still need to evaluate the stocks. Most stocks with bad fundamentals will not appreciate. However there are examples on turnaround situations (some call them catalysts) such as:

- A new drug has positive test result.
- A new product.
- A new discovery or breakthrough.
- Being acquired.
- Being settled with a major lawsuit.

Screen stocks first and then analyze the screened stocks one by one.

The most updated information is from the Earning Conference Call (easier to obtain it from SeekingAlpha), Q10 report and from the company's web site. Finviz.com seems to be more updated than most other sites besides the above.

When to sell a stock? I have three chapters at the end of this section. They are in the same topic but in different approaches / concepts.

The better analysis gives you better chance of success, but as everything in life there is no guarantee.

1   Simplest way to evaluate stocks

Beginners should trade ETFs only. This chapter is for the readers who are ready or getting ready to trade stocks.

Many stock researches have already been done recently and some are available free of charge. I have no affiliation with Fidelity except I retired from it. You can open an account with them with no balance. Their Equity Summary Score is one of the best indicators; I check out **value** stocks with score higher than 8.

Several sources

The popular ones are Morningstar, Value Line, The Street and Zacks (currently free for rankings of individual stocks). If they are not free, check out whether they are available from your local library. I have 3 simple ways to evaluate stocks starting with the simplest. In addition, read the articles on the selected stocks from Fidelity, Finviz, Seeking Alpha and many other sources for further evaluation.

Fidelity

Select only stocks that have Fidelity's Equity Summary Score 8 or higher. There are tons of information about a stock.

A modified stock selection based on a magazine article

Most metrics are available from Finviz.

1. Forward P/E (expected earnings and not based on the last twelve months). It should range from 5 to 15 (10 to 25 for high tech stocks). EV/EBITDA (from Yahoo!Finance) is a better choice as it includes the debts and cash than P/E; it would be more effective if it uses forward earnings. If you do not use EV/EBITDA, ensure Debt/Equity is less than 0.5 except for the debt-intensive industries.

2. ROE (Return of Equity) measures how well the company uses the capital. I prefer stocks with ROE greater than 5%.

3. Volatility. Conservative investors should select stocks with a beta of less than one (i.e. less volatile).

4. Insider Transactions from should be less than 5%.

5. Momentum. Check out the SMA-50 (actually SMA-50%) and SMA-200. Ideally they should be positive. It is especially important for stocks you do not want to keep for a long time.

A simple scoring system using Finviz

Bring up Finviz.com and then enter the stock symbol.

No.	Metric	Good	Bad	Score
1	Forward P/E[1]	Between 2.5 and 12.5, Score = 2	> 50 or < 0, Score = -1	
2	P/ FCF[1]	< 12, Score = 1	>30 or < 0, Score = -1	
3	P/S[1]	< 0.8, Score = 1	< 0, Score = -1	
4	P/ B[1]	< 1, Score = 1	< 0, Score = -1	
	Compare quarter to quarter of last year			
5	Sales Q/Q	> 15%, Score = 1	< 0, Score = -1	
6	EPS Q/Q	> 20%, Score = 1	< 0, Score = -1	
			Grand Score	
	Stock Symbol Date[2]	Current Price	SPY	

Footnote

[1] Negative values for Sales (due to accounting adjustments), Equity and Book are possible but not likely.

[2] The last row is for your information only. SPY is used to measure whether it will beat the market by comparing the return of this stock to the return of SPY.

The Score

Score each metric and sum up all the scores giving the Grand Score. If the Grand Score is 3, the stock passes this scoring system. Even if it is a 2, it still deserves further analysis if you have time. You may want to add scores from other vendors. To illustrate on using Fidelity, add 1 to the score if Fidelity's Equity Summary score is 8 or higher. Monitor the performance after every 6 months or so to see whether this scoring system beats the market.

Very basic advice for beginners

Beginners should stick with U.S. stocks with Market Cap greater than 800 M (million), Debt/Equity less than .25 (25%) except for debt-intensive industries such as utilities and airlines and Forward P/E between 5 to 20 (25 for high-tech companies). These metrics are all available from Finviz.com, which is free.

Do not have more than 20% of your portfolio in one stock (unless it is an ETF or mutual fund) and do not have more than 30% of your portfolio in one sector.

For more conservative investors, buy non-volatile stocks whose beta (available from Yahoo!Finance) is less than 1. Beta of 1 represents the market (the S&P 500 index). For example, a stock with beta 1.5 statistically fluctuates more than 50% of the market and hence it is very volatile.

Try paper trading to check out your strategy and your skill in trading stocks. If your broker does not provide one, use a spreadsheet to record your trades or check the availability of simulator.investopedia.com.

Filler 12 noon is not 12 pm

The Chinese restaurant I went to says they are open at 12 am. Are they wrong or is the world wrong?

The next hour after 11 am is 12 am, NOT 12 pm. The one who set it up did it totally wrong and no one complains about it until now. If I were born earlier, I would have corrected it.

2   Finviz parameters

Most metrics are described in Finviz(via Help), Investopedia and/or Wikipedia and my chapter on P/E. The following are my personal comments and why I feel some metrics are more important than others. Compare the ratios to the companies in the same sector and also its averages from the last 5 years.

From your browser, enter Finviz.com. Enter a symbol (I used ABEO for discussion). A chart is displayed with the prices and volumes for the last nine months. SMAs (Single Moving Average) are displayed sometimes with other technical indicators. Intraday, Daily and Weekly options are available.

Besides the metrics described next and the chart, it describes what the company does, analysts' recommendations (I prefer Fidelity's Equity Summary), insiders' trading and articles that are good for qualitative analysis. "Financial Highlights and Statements" are materials for more in-depth analysis and they were more important decades ago when most financial ratios had not been calculated for you.

The following metrics are roughly based on the flow of Finviz from top to bottom and left to right. I skip those metrics that I believe are not too important. You can also place your cursor on the metric to have the description from Finviz. Some metrics are left blank when they are zero or negative. For example, the Debt/Equity of YRCW in 1/2019 is blank (same as null) due to Equity being negative. From Yahoo!Finance, it has a total debt of 888M.

- **Index**. Most of us trade stocks in the three major exchanges in the USA. Stocks listed over-the-counter are too risky for most of us. Skip the stocks in local exchanges and foreign exchanges if you are not an expert on these stocks. I screen the stocks and then ignore the stocks that are not in the Dow, NASDAC and Amex.

- **Market Cap** (MC). To me, stocks below 50M are risky even they could be very profitable. Ensure the Avg. Volume is at least 10,000 shares and / or your order is less than 1% of the average volume. Some small stocks are controlled by the owners and have small volumes. In this case you cannot sell your stock easily.

Float = Outstanding shares – Insider shares.

Usually it does not matter as they are typically the same. However, it does for small companies with large insider shares. Most of these owners do not want to sell their family businesses and hence they reduce the chance of being acquired entirely or partly for good prices.

- If **Forward P/E** (a.k.a. Expected P/E) is not provided, use the P/E which is based on the last 12 months. Alternatively, calculate the E by using the E from P/E and multiplying it by its growth rate. It may not be seasonally adjusted. I prefer Expected P/E (or called Forward P/E) as it provides a better predictability power from my limited research.

  Finviz.com leaves the P/E and some other metrics blank if the earnings are negative.

  Compare the P/E or Forward P/E with the average P/E for the sector and its average P/E for the last 5 years that are available from Fidelity.com. Some sectors have high P/Es. If the sector is cyclical, the earnings could be affected.

- **Cash / share**. It is used to calculate Pow P/E and Pow EY. To illustrate, if the stock is $10 and it has $10 cash / share without debt (i.e. Debt/Equity = 0), most likely it is underpriced as you can get the whole company for nothing. You should find out why the price is so low.

- **Dividend %** is useful for income investors. The payout ratio should not be more than 30% except for matured companies.

- **Recs**. Select stocks with 1 or 2. Do not base your stock selection on this recommendation alone. There have been many bad recommendations that could cost you a fortune in losses.

- **PEG** is a measure of the growth of P/E and hence a growth metric. The lower is better if earnings are positive. If earnings are negative, then the reverse is true. It is a defect in using P/E and PEG and that's why I recommend EY (Earnings Yield), earnings yield, and EYG, earnings yield growth.

If there are two companies with the same P/E, the one with a better PEG ratio is better. If two companies have the same E/P, the company with higher Earnings Growth (EPS Q/Q) would be favorable.

- **P/B**. Book value (= Total Assets − Total Liabilities) may not include intangible asset such as patents. Do not trust it 100%, so is ROE which is based on book value. Negative equity is possible when Total Liabilities is more than Total Assets.

- **P/S**. If two companies are unprofitable, this ratio can be used. I prefer profitable companies.

- **P/FCF**. I prefer it to be greater than 0 and less than 50 for value investors. Most metrics can be manipulated easily, but not this one.

- **Sales Q/Q** reduces the seasonal deviation. To illustrate, retail sales for the Christmas season should be compared it to the same season in prior year.

- **EPS Q/Q**. Same as above. I prefer the growth of EPS over Sales. The Q/Q ratios are growth metrics. When a company terminates its unprofitable product(s), its Sales Q/Q could be down but its EPS Q/Q could be up. In 2000, many internet companies had great Sales Q/Qs but negative EPS Q/Qs.

  Q/Q comparison (quarter to quarter) takes out the seasonal variations.

  When the company buys its own shares, EPS could be misleading as E is fixed and the number of shares is reduced.

- Positive **Insider** Transactions are favorable. So is Institutional Transactions as institutional investors move the market.

- Insider Own, Shares Outstanding and Shares **Float** determine the number of shares that are available for trading. A small Float with a high Insider Own limits trading and the stock should be avoided in most cases. Compare your trade position for the stock to the Avg. Volume.

- **Profit Margin**. I prefer it over Gross Margin and Oper. Margin which does not include interest expenses and taxes. When you sell software, the Gross Margin is high as it does not include development, support and marketing, etc. A retail store has low Gross Margin.

- **Short Float**. I prefer it to be less than 10%. If it is greater than 10%, the shorters could find something wrong with the company. If it is over 25%, I would check the fundamentals. If they are good, I would buy expecting a short squeeze potential. It has been risky but proven to be profitable for me.

- Technical metrics: **SMA-20**, SMA-50 and SMA-200. If they are all positive, it means the trend is good. SMA-20 is short-term trend and SMA-200 is a long-term trend. If you are short-term swing investor, stick with short-term trend and vice versa. The first two are momentum grades.

- **RSI(14)**. If it greater than 60% (some use 65%), it is overbought. If it is under 30% (some use 25%), it is under bought. Use it as a reference. Most stocks making new heights are always overbought.

- **Beta**. A volatile stock fluctuates a lot. It is good for short-term traders. A beta of 1 means the stock would fluctuate with the market and more volatile if it is higher than 1.

- Management performance is measured by **ROA.** It is also judged by **Analysts' Rec.** and Institutional Ownership (except for small companies). The confidence of their own ability, the company and its sector is measured by Insider Ownership and Insider Purchases.

- Avoid all bankrupting companies at all cost. Debt/Equity, P/FCF, Cash/Sh., P/B, Profit Margin, Forward P/E, Short Float, RSI(14), SMA20% and SMA50 would give us hints. Need to summarize all the info and study many other factors such as obsoleting products (including drugs).

- Unless you have concrete information, do not buy stocks a week or so before the Earnings Date.

More useful information:

- The price chart. It has a lot of features such as the resistance line. Some charts include technical indicators such as double top (a bearish warning) and double bottom (a bullish sign).
- Description under the symbol. It briefly describes what the company (sector and industry) does and its country of registration. You want to buy a stock within a sector that is trending up. For example according to Finviz, Apple is in the Consumer Goods sector and the Electronic Equipment industry.

  If you do not want to buy foreign stocks, skip it if it is not listed in the US exchange.
- Articles on the company for qualitative analysis.
- Insider trading. Pay more attention to the insider purchases at market prices. Use common sense.
- The last line lets you open Yahoo!Finance and other sites.

Your broker's web site

Your broker web site should have plenty of tools to analyze stocks. As of Dec., 2018, Fidelity lets you use their extensive research free by opening an account with no position restriction. I describe some of their metrics that should be beneficial to your research.

- Equity Summary Score. Potentially good buy when it is 7 (8 for conservative investors) or higher. With some exceptions, you should avoid or short stocks if the score is 3 or below. The stocks ranking from 4 to 6 could be turnaround candidates if they are supported by good Q/Q Earnings and/or good news.

- The 5-year averages are good yardsticks. For example, in Dec., 2018, C's P/E is about 9 and the average is 14. Hence it is a value buy.

Other sources

If you have other sources (most require a subscription or being a customer), skip the stocks that have one of the failing grades. The exceptions are a new positive development and increased insider purchases.

Vendor	Grade	Fail
Fidelity	Equity Summary Score	< 7
IBD	Composite grade	< 50
Value Line	Proj. 3-5 yr. return. Also its composite rating	< 3%
Zacks	Rank	5
Vector Vest	VST	< 0.7

You may be able to find Value Line and IBD in your library. Try out the free stock reports from your broker first. Finviz and Seeking Alpha should have articles (now fewer free articles from Seeking Alpha) on stocks and earnings conferences, which could have important information after separating from the "welcome" and garbage talks.

Yahoo!Finance has good info. "EV/EBITDA" is better than "P/E" as it considers debts and cash. Most use Earnings from last 12 months, which has poorer predictability than Forward Earnings to me.

When negative values such as Equity in Finviz.com, we need to adjust many related metrics or do not use them at all.

MarketWatch.com has many articles on the market in general and personal investing.

If the stock is closed to the Earnings Date (found in Finviz.com), you should avoid trading the stock; as earnings could have a big swing for the stock price. Consult Zacks' ranking which is currently free for individual stocks.

Gurus

It is nice to know how gurus would rate the interested stocks. GuruFocus is a good source. NASDAQ is a simplified version, but it is currently free. Bring up Nasdaq.com from your browser. Select "Investing" and then "Guru Screeners". On the third selection, enter the stock symbol such as THO. Click "Go". You will find how 10 or so gurus would evaluate this stock in theory. Click "Detailed Analysis" for each guru.

5-minute stock evaluation.

- From Finviz.com, enter the stock or ETF symbol. Look at the number of reds in metrics. If there have more than greens, most likely it is not a good stock.

- Check out Forward P/E (E>0 and P/E < 20), Debut / Equity (< 50%) and P/FCF (not in red color).

  If time is allowed, replace Forward P/E with True P/E (same as "EV/EBITDA"), which is available from Yahoo!Finance and other sources.

- SMA20 (or SMA50 for longer holding period). If SMA20 is > 10%, it is trending up.

- It is fine if the Insider Transaction is positive.

  If you have more time, scroll down for Insider Trade. It usually is a good buy if insiders are buying it recently and heavily with the current market prices.

- Be cautious on foreign stocks and low-volume stocks.

- If most of the above are positive, it is likely a buy. As in life, nothing is 100% certain.

Links
PEG: http://en.wikipedia.org/wiki/PEG_ratio
Short %:
http://www.investopedia.com/university/shortselling/shortselling1.asp#axzz2LNDvpemo
Openinsider: http://www.openinsider.com/
Finviz: http://Finviz.com/
terms: http://www.Finviz.com/help/screener.ashx
Insider Cow: http://www.insidercow.com/
Current Ratio: http://en.wikipedia.org/wiki/Current_ratio
How to find quality stocks.
http://seekingalpha.com/article/2381395-how-to-identify-quality-stocks-and-is-there-really-alpha-to-be-had

3   Intangibles

I give a score for each stock I evaluate. Occasionally some stocks with poor scores have great returns and vice versa. In general, the scoring system works. It has been proven statistically and repeatedly from my limited data. I stick with high-score stocks with some exceptions.

Once in a while I change my scoring system to adept to the current market conditions. To illustrate, the market bottom phase and early recovery phase of the market cycle favor value more than momentum/growth. Here are some of my recent experiences and strategies:

- I double or even triple my stake on stocks with high scores. In the longer term, they are consistently better winners than the average with some minor exceptions. Besides the score, look at the intangibles described in this article.

- Watch out for the stocks with outrageous metrics such as P/E of 4 or less. It could be a big lawsuit pending, an expiration of some important drugs, etc. Also, be careful with scores in the top 5%. From my statistics they do worse than the average. Their problems may not show up in the current financial statements.

- The technology of a tech company cannot be ignored even though the company's P/E is high, that I set a limit of 25 instead of 20 for other stocks. The value of the company's technology and patents will not be shown in the fundamental metrics except from the insiders' purchases at market prices.

  For example, IDCC rose about 40% in 2 days. There was a rumor that Google was buying the company and/or Apple was bidding on it too for its mobile technology. Charts usually would flag this kind of event. For non-charters, use the SMA-20% from Finviz.com. They could be a little late as the charts depend on rising prices.

- There are more acquisitions during a market bottom (same as early recovery). The companies with good technologies are bargains and the larger companies especially those in the same sector understand their values better than most of us. These potentially profitable companies will not be shown by their scores explicitly. When corporations have a lot of cash or the credit is cheap, they are looking for smaller companies to acquire or invest in. The candidates are usually small, beaten up, low-priced and having valuable intangible assets such as technologies, customer base and/or market share of the industry segment. 2009-2012 was just the perfect environment and the before that was 2003. I had at least one stock in each of these periods and they appreciated a lot.

- The opposite is Netflix, Chipotle in 1/2012 and Amazon in 1/2013. They are over-priced by any measure. However, the mentioned companies are investing in the future. The shorters (not for beginners) are having a tough time in making money on them. When their P/Es are higher than 40, watch out. Some could be OK in the mentioned companies, but usually they are not. Do not follow the herd and your due diligence will verify whether they will still go up.

  Use reward/risk ratio. It is based on experiences. To illustrate, if the company has the equal chance to go up 50% and go down 25%, then it is a buy and the reverse is a sell.

- The retail investor just cannot possibly know about some events until they actually happen. For example, ATSC dropped 15% due to losing its second primary customer. Fundamentals cannot predict this kind of events. Charts can signal this event, but usually they are too late unless you watch the chart all day long.

- After a quick run up, TZOO plunged due to missing some negligible earning expectations. It seems the original climbing prices already had the perfect earnings growth built-in.

  I do not understand why a company loses 10% of its market cap when it missed by 1% of the expected earnings. It could be driven up and down by the institutional investors. Evaluate the stock before you act. Acting opposite to the institutional investors could be very profitable for the right stocks. Avoid trading before the earnings announcement dates (about 4 times a year for most stocks).

- The following are not easily found in financial statements: industry outlook, patents, good will, market share, competition, product margins, management quality, lawsuits pending, potential acquisition, pension obligations, advertising icons, etc. That is why we need to read articles on the stocks in our buy list or our purchased stocks.

- The financial data could be fraudulent or manipulated. I do not trust small companies in emerging markets. I have been burned too many times. Check the company names such as foreign names, ADR and their headquarter addresses (from the company profile in most investing sites).

  Earnings can be manipulated with many accounting tricks. A jump in earnings from last year may not be as rosy as it looks. Check the footnotes in the accounting statements. I usually skip financial statements unless I have big purchases in mind as my time in investing is limited.

- Cash flow cannot be easily manipulated. It is good information whether the company will survive or not, but to me it does not prove to be a consistent predictor in my tests, but an important red flag for companies on their way to bankruptcy. Examples abound.

- Repeated one-time, non-recurring and extraordinary charges are red flags.

- Stay away from the companies where the CEOs are over-compensated. As of 7- 2013, Activision's CEO raised his salary by more than 600%, while the stock lost its value in double digits.

- Value stocks. Need to know why they become value stocks (i.e. fewer investors want to own) even they are financially sound. For example, there are two primary reasons for the downfall of a supplier to Apple: 1. Apple is declining in sales and 2. Apple is switching suppliers to replace their product. Technology companies are continually building better mouse traps. They could turn around in a year or so with better products.

Conclusion

Buying a stock is an educated guess that its stock price will rise. Fundamentals do not always work, but they work most of the time:

1. When we buy a value stock, we're swimming against the tide. Hence, we need to wait longer (usually more than 6 months) for the market to realize its value. The exception is the Early Recovery phase (see the

Market Cycle chapter) and it has faster and larger returns than most other stocks from most other stages of the market cycle.

2. Some metrics are misleading. Book value could be misleading for an established company such as IBM. The image of the cowboy in a tobacco company could be a very important asset that is not included in its financial statement.

3. The market is not always rational.

Afterthoughts

- Brand names of big companies are one of the most important intangibles. Here is a strategy to buy big companies in a down market. It has been proven that it works. However, do not just buy these companies without analysis.
http://seekingalpha.com/article/1324041-buying-brand-names-in-a-bear-market-can-make-you-rich

- The reputation of a company takes a long time to build but a bad incidence to destroy in the case of GM such as the delay in recalling the killer switches.

#Filler: Carrie Fisher, another sad American story

Unless drug addiction is part of the culture now as evidenced from the legalization of certain drugs, we're in a permissive society! Brits pushed opium as a nation when they had nothing better to trade. Opium killed millions of Chinese and bankrupted China. When we do not learn from history, we will repeat history. It is another sad story of fame and money and then losing it all. I bet she would be happier in a normal life instead of being born in a privileged class. Same can be said for many celebrities such as Presley, Houston and her daughter. RIP.

4   Qualitative analysis

This is the last analysis to evaluate a stock fundamentally. Then the next is technical analysis which is used to find an entry point (also the exit point) for the stock.

Where quantitative analysis fails and why

I find that some stocks with high scores fail and some stocks with low scores succeed as indicated by my performance monitor. The scoring system still works statistically for the majority of my stocks.

- Reasons why stocks with low scores perform in addition to the described in the last discussion:

  - Over-sold. The institutional investors (fund managers and pension managers) dump them first, and then followed by the retail investors. These big boys will buy these stocks back when they reach a certain price range. RSI(14), a technical indicator described in the Technical Analysis article, is useful to detect these over-sold stocks. This metric is readily available from many sites including Finviz.

  - The falling price (P) improves all fundamental metrics that have the stock price such as P/E and P/Sales. However, the trend of the price is down.

  - The company has turned around after fixing its problems and/or the market has changed for the better.

  - The current problems have been resolved but not known to the public. It includes resolving a lawsuit, a new product, a new drug, or a new big order, etc.

  - Heavy purchases by insiders. The company's outlook is not shown in its financial statements. Sometimes the insiders hide them so they can buy more of their companies' stocks for themselves.

- Reasons why stocks with high scores plunge in addition to the described in the previous discussion:

- o   The company's fundamentals and its prices have reached or closed to the maximum heights. They have no way to go but down. It is particularly true when the stock's timing rating is at or close to the highest point. TTWO that I gifted to my grandchildren had been 5-baggers in the last few years before it plunged in 2018.

- o   It has reached its potential value (or a target price) and it is time for many investors to take profits.

- o   Sector (or stock) rotation, particularly by institutional investors who drive the market.

- o   The outlook of the company, its sector and/or the market is deteriorating.

- o   The stock price may be manipulated. There are many reasons to pump and dump the stock. Shorting is not recommended for most investors. However, some experienced shorters make money consistently when they find valid reasons to short stocks.

- o   It could be due to a new serious lawsuit, a new competing product or drug, canceling a major order, etc.

- o   Downgrade by analysts. They could spot some bad events such as product defects, violations of regulations or accounting errors / frauds. The downgrades are more important than the upgrades that could have conflict of interest.

- o   The financial statement had been manipulated. The SEC may ask for an investigation.

- o   Does not meet the consensus in earnings announcements, which have been over-acted by many investors.

Qualitative Analysis

We need to do further analysis after the quantitative analysis and the intangible analysis. Check out the company's prospects. Check out the date of the article and any potential hidden agenda items from the author. Older articles may not have much value.

Be careful on 'pump-and-dump' manipulation written by authors with a hidden agenda. It has happened especially on small companies before even SeekingAlpha.com has its share. Here was an article that tells you to sell NHTC. There was another article to tell you to buy ARTX. They fit into this category.

The sources are:

1. Seeking Alpha.
   Type the symbol of the company to read as many articles on the company as you have time for. Today this site and many other similar sites require you to be a paid member. If you cannot find too many good articles, check out the articles from Finviz.com.

   Recently, I read an article on AMD and it said it may have good profits in the next two years with the game consoles. The outlook of a company is not shown by any fundamental metric which are far from favorable.

   Following a well-known writer, I bought IBM without doing my due diligence (my fault). It went down more than 15% quickly. You can learn from my mistakes.

2. Research reports from your broker. If you do not find many, open an account with one that provides such reports. Some subscription services such as Value Line provide such reports.

3. Yahoo!Finance board. Most comments are garbage. However, once in a while you find some great insights. Usually you cannot find any info from other sources on tiny companies.

4. The most recent company's financial statements. They are usually available in the company's web site.

5. 10-Ks from Edgar database (www.sec.gov/edgar). Check out new products and its potential competition, key customers, order backlog, research and development and pending lawsuits.

6. Check out the outlook of the sector the company is in and the company itself.

7. Check out its competitors.

8. Some companies are run by stupid people. I received information via my email saying that my mutual fund account could be treated as an abandoned property. I have been cashing dividend checks every year and why it would be considered as an abandoned property. I called them right away to close my account.

    The tall and handsome guy presented articulately how he would turn around JC Penny on TV. I could tell you right away that all his tricks had been tried by other companies such as Sears, and most did not work. The intelligent investor does not care about how handsome, how articulated, how rich his family is and how many advanced degrees from prestigious colleges he possesses. If he does not make sense, do not buy his preaching and his company's stock. [Update. As of 5/2020, J.C. Penny filed for bankruptcy protection. If you had this stock and my book, you would have saved a lot of money minus $10 for my book!]

9. Check out its business model. Some business models do not make business sense and some do. Here are some samples.

*   Giving razors makes sense, as the customers have to buy the blades eventually and keep on buying blades for life.

*   Supermarket M lowers prices on common merchandises such as Coke and it works. They make money by providing inferior (but profitable to them) products that you cannot compare prices easily such as meat and seafood.

    Eventually there will be a supermarket in my area to satisfy me both in price and quality or at least make a good tradeoff.

*   Last week it had been brutally hot. I went to a Barns & Noble's bookstore to enjoy reading the updated books and enjoyed the air conditioning. When there are more free loaders like me than customers, this business model does not work.

*   Market dumping works to capture the market. Microsoft used to do it with their new Office and Mail products that could not compete with the established products at the time. Google is following the same

model to dump its equivalent products to compete with Office. Now, Microsoft is taking a dose of the same medicine. As of 2015, Google is not winning.

Amazon.com gives writers (like myself) great deals if you only sell your digital books via them. This model will work so far, as it has captured the self-publishing market today.

5   When to sell a stock

There are many reasons to sell a stock as follows.

Personal
1. Has met my targets/objectives.
    It could be a 10% gain in a very short-term swing, x% return in 4 months for a short-term swing or y% gain after a year for long-term trades. Define x and y depending on your risk tolerance and how often you trade.

    I bought 4 stocks in one day during the August, 2015 correction and placed sell orders with 10% more than my purchase prices. I sold one in a day and another one within a month. This is my strategy for correction – sometimes it works and sometimes it does not.

    Never look back. Do not blame yourself when the prices are better than your trade prices. When the market is volatile, use a higher percent of the current prices. Be disciplined. Stay on the same strategy and detach yourself from emotions.

2. Realize that we have made a mistake. Do not let your ego block your eyes. It could be due to bad analysis, bad, data, unexpected fraud, lawsuits, and/or unforeseeable events that you have no control of. It is better to get out with a small loss. I prefer a 25% loss as a threshold for long-term strategies and a 10% (or less for some strategies) loss for short-term strategies.

    We have to ensure whether it is a mistake or not. If the 'mistake' is just bad luck or due to conditions we cannot possibly predict or control, then it is not a mistake. If it is a mistake, learn from it. When we diversify, one bad loss should not cause a big dent in our portfolios. The stop loss is a good tool most of the time except when there is a flash crash.

If the criteria have been faithfully followed and it does not work well, check out whether your criteria are wrong, or it does not work on the current market conditions.

3. When we have too many stocks in the same sector, we will want to replace some stocks to better diversify our portfolios.

   When the sector is rising, we want to weigh more on that sector at the expense of diversification, and vice versa. Set a limit of how many sectors you should hold.

4. Need cash for living expenses.

5. To reduce a tax burden by selling some losers. Tax consideration should not be the primary reason for selling. Take advantage of the favorable tax treatment for long-term capital gains. In short, sell losers within the short term limit (currently a year), and sell winners after 365 days; check the current tax laws.

   Harvest tax losses. Sell losers and buy back similar stocks (or same stock after 31 days to avoid wash sale). It is not too clear in which you can buy back the same loser in your children's account under the current tax law.

6. To take advantage of a lower tax. In 2013, we can pay virtually zero (except the increase of tax on social security payment) Federal income taxes on long-term capital gains when our income is below a specific tax bracket (15% as of 2015). Check out the current tax laws. Evaluate the sold winners for a possible buy back.

Market Timing
7. When the market or the sector plunges, sell stocks or stocks within the sector.

   For temporary peaks, evaluate which stocks in your portfolio to sell based on fundamentals. The objective is to raise cash for buying opportunities.

Deteriorating appreciation potential
8. There may be some stocks that have a better appreciation potential than the ones you currently own. Churning the portfolio by replacing

better stocks may cost some brokerage commissions (some are free today) and taxes for taxable accounts, but it improves the quality and the appreciation potential for the entire portfolio.

9. The company's fundamentals have changed for the worse. If you use a scoring system, compare the current score with the score you actually bought the stock for. Apple is a good example from 2013 to 2015. Buy when the fundamentals are good and sell when they are not.

   The basic fundamentals are expected P/E, the quarter-to-quarter earnings growth rate / the sales growth rate, and Debt /Equity.

   When your stocks have passed the peak and started to decline, sell them. When they are heading to bankruptcy, sell them fast.

Hints that the fundamentals are degrading

Evaluate the stocks you own at least every 6 months and check their daily news at least once a week that can be easily done using Seeking Alpha's portfolio function.

- The cash flow is decreasing fast. Cash flow is not a particularly good predicative indicator for appreciation, but a good indicator on whether the company will survive. This metric is very hard to manipulate.

- A new or pending lawsuit. Check out how serious the lawsuit is and be aware that a minor lawsuit can be ignored. Companies always sue against each other.

- A big drop in sales. Do not be alarmed when a new product, or a new drug is going to replace a major product. Compare sales to the same quarter of prior year to avoid seasonal fluctuations (Q-to-Q info I available from Finviz.com).

- Management deteriorates- One hint is the deteriorating ROE from the last quarter.

- The extravagant life style of the CEO and the many easy loans to officers.

- Poor operations. They include recalls of products such as the GM recall on ignition switches, product secrets being stolen and customers' credit card info being stolen. Boeing's 747-Max is a warning call.

- A successful product from the competitor, or the current product is losing its market share, or becoming a low-profit commodity.

- Insiders and/or institutional investors are dumping the companies' stocks far more than the averages (2% for me) especially in heavy volumes and by more than one insider.

  - Have more than one insider dumping a lot of the stock within a month and no insider purchase in that month.

  - Have more than one insider decrease their holdings by more than 10%.

- When the SEC or any government agency pays attention to a company, it usually means bad news.

- Deceptive accounting practices have been discovered.

- Increasing receivable and/or inventory at an alarming rate.

- Earnings have been restated too many times.

- Short percentage is increasing fast – someone found something wrong with the company.

- The invalidity of 'one-time charges'.

- Abnormal return rate of the company's pension fund comparing to the average of the companies in the same sector.

- Too many and too costly reconstructing charges.

- The entire stock market is plunging as indicated by our chart in detecting market crashes.

- The stock price does not move up with good news. It shows the price has peaked.

- The accumulation amount is far less than the sold amount. When the stock price is up, the accumulation is less than the sold stocks when the stock price was down the last time. It indicates that no more accumulation is ahead and hence the stock will be down most likely.

Afterthoughts

- Another article on this topic.
  http://buzz.money.cnn.com/2013/04/05/stocks-sell/
  An article from Investopedia. Nothing new but it is worth having the same second opinion.
  http://www.investopedia.com/financial-edge/0412/5-tips-on-when-to-sell-your-stock.aspx

- It also depends on your strategies. I sell most of my stocks in my momentum portfolio within a month. At least one strategy I know of does not keep any stock during the peak stage of the market cycle — the easiest time to make money but also the riskiest time.

  If you use charts for trading, sell the stocks that are below your moving averages or other technical analysis indicators. Personally I do not use charts for making sell decisions due to my limited time.

- Sell when the company is heading into bankruptcy as described before. The red flags are: 1. Negative cash flow. 2. Heavy insiders dumping the stocks. 3. Pending major lawsuit. 4. Fraud from the management.

- Risky periods for a stock.
  Earnings announcement (4 times a year), settling a major lawsuit and/or during a FDA event in approving a drug are risky periods for a stock. A fluctuation more than 5% in either direction is normal. Some use options to buy insurance. Most ignore it. For the majority of the time, heavy insider purchase is a good indicator. There are rumors (or educated guesses) on earnings before their announcements. Zacks is supposed to be a good subscription for earnings estimates.

6   Sectors to be cautious with

There are many reasons to be very cautious when investing in the following sectors. However, Technical Analysis (a.k.a. charting) would give you more hints than the fundamentals for stocks for these sectors. If the big guys are dumping, most likely Technical Analysis (or the simplest SMA-20) would tell you that.

Loan companies/banks

The financial statements do not show the quality of their loan portfolios. Following this advice, you may be able to skip the banks that melted down in 2007. The peak of Citigroup is $550 and several banks went bankrupt.

Drug (generic is ok)

Understanding the complexities of the drug pipelines, its potential profits for new drugs and the expiration of the current drugs may not worth the effort for most retail investors. In addition, a serious lawsuit and / or a serious problem with a drug could wipe out a good percentage of the stock price. When a drug shows unpromising sign(s) in any trial phase, the stock could plunge and vice versa.

Miners

It is extremely difficult to estimate how much ore (sometimes a miner owns several different types of ores and/or of different grades in the same or different mines) that a company has. It is further complicated by the complexities to extract and transport them. When the total of these costs is greater than its production price, the company will not be profitable. Understanding the market for ore futures is another discipline.

Many mining companies are in foreign countries such as Canada, Australia and countries in South America. Their financial statements of Canada and Australia are more trustworthy than most other emerging countries.

One potential problem of mining companies from many emerging countries is nationalization.

Mining rare earth ore is extremely risky when the profit depends on how China, a major producer of these ores, will price these ores. After China announced the export restrictions on rare earth elements, several non-Chinese companies announced to reopen their mines for rare earths, but few have made any profits as of 2013. Developed countries have stricter environmental regulations.

Coal and eventually oil suffer from the rising use of cleaner energy such as solar and wind.

Insurance companies

Insurance companies profit by:

1. The difference between the total premiums received and the total claims minus expenses in running the company.

2. How well they invest the premiums; you pay your premiums earlier than you may collect from any claims.

They can protect the profits in #1 by restricting claims by natural disasters such as earthquakes and by re-insuring. However, a bad disaster could wipe out a lot of their profits.

Even if the insurance company shows you its investment portfolio, most of us, the retail investors, do not have the time and expertise to analyze it.

Emerging countries (not a sector)

Their financial statements especially from small companies cannot be trusted, and many countries use different accounting standards. Emerging countries are where the economic growth is. I trade FXI, an ETF, rather than individual Chinese companies. I have lost a lot in small Chinese companies due to frauds and politics. To check out whether the stock is an ADR, try ADR.COM (https://www.adr.com/).

Stocks with low volumes (not a sector)

Most likely you pay a high spread to trade these stocks. They can be manipulated easier. I had a hard time trying to sell a stock owned by a few owners.

For simplicity, I trade stocks with the average daily trade volume over 6,000 shares (double it if the price is $2 or less). A better way could be by calculating the percent of your trade quantity / average daily trade volume; it would reduce the effect of penny stocks that have larger volumes due to the low prices.

Good business and bad business

Banking is a good business in a growing economy. My deposit in them makes virtually zero interest, and they loan the same money making 3%. If they are more cautious in loaning, they should make good profits.

Restaurant is an easy business to run, but it is very hard to make good money. With the rising of minimal wages, it will get even tougher. That could be the reason for so many coupons today. The high-end restaurants are doing better due to the rising stock market. The pandemic of 2020 would wipe out a lot of small restaurants.

Retailing is a tough business. Look at the top 10 retailers 15 years ago, I can only find two including Macy's that are still surviving. Most are either went bankrupt or being acquired. Even Macy's was not in good financial shape. Amazon is the killer.

Airlines are a tough business. You can tell by the average increase in fares in the last 10 years. It cannot even beat inflation. They have to charge you for everything. The next frontier charge is the rest room (especially for long-distance flights). Now I understand why they call themselves "Frontier Air". As of 2014, it is quite profitable due to mergers and lower fuel cost. The pandemic of 2020 may be the toughest time for airlines. As of 5/2020, Boeing has many serious troubles and they can only survive with a bailout from the government.

There are several software companies that produce software such as the virus detecting programs and tax preparation software. The customers faithfully buy new versions every year. That's great business.

Afterthoughts
As of 8/2013, is the emerging market oversold?
http://seekingalpha.com/article/1658252-have-emerging-markets-gotten-oversold

Section III: Market timing

Investing from 1970 to 2000 enjoys an average annual return of about 10% and market timing is a waste of time and actually reduces the performance by parking too much cash. Since 2000, the market has changed. As of 5/2014, we have two major market plunges with an average loss of over 45%.

The apples you picked are sour but some other times are tasty from the same tree. You just pick them in the wrong time or in the right time.

Market timing is about educated guesses unless you have a time machine. Hopefully we will have more rights than wrongs when we follow general guidelines. It would reduce risk and could benefit us financially in the long run.

The following chapter helps you to time the market in the simplest term. It is followed by several related chapters. Just the first one and try it out. Skip the rest in section for now.

Tip

	SMA-50	SMA-200	SMA-350	SMA50/ SMA200	RSI (14)
Market					
Peak		5%	9%	101%	65%
Bottom		-32%	-31%	78%	25%
Correction					
Peak	4%	6%	11%	102%	65%
Bottom	-5%	-6%	-7%	97%	26%
Stock					
Peak					70%
Bottom					30%

SMA350% = (Stock Price – SMA) / SMA
where SMA is Single Moving Average for 350 sessions

1   Simplest market timing

Market timing depends on charts; the following describes how to use chart information without creating charts. Most charts will not identify the peaks and bottoms of the market as they depend on data (i.e. the stock prices). However, it would reduce further loses. It is simpler than it sounds. Just follow the procedure below.

The first part of this technique detects market plunges, and the second part advises you when to reenter the market. I have modified them.

How to detect market plunges without charts (a.k.a. <u>Death Cross</u>)

1. Bring up Finviz.com.

2. Enter SPY (or any ETF that simulates the market).

3. If SMA-200% is positive, it indicates that the market plunge has not been detected and you can skip the following steps.

4. The market is plunging if SMA-50% is more negative than SMA-200%. To illustrate this condition, SMA-200% is -2% and SMA-50% is -5%.

5. Sell most stocks starting with the riskiest ones first such as the ones with negative earnings, high P/Es and/or high Debt/Equity. Obtain this info from Finviz.com by entering the symbol of the stock you own.

6. Conservative investors should sell only those over-priced stocks. Aggressive investors should sell all stocks. Extremely aggressive investors should sell all stocks, buy contra ETFs, and even short stocks. I do not recommend beginners to be aggressive.

When to return to the market (a.k.a. <u>Golden Cross</u>)

Use the above in a reversed sense to detect whether the market has been recovering. However, when the SMA-200% turns positive, I would start buying value stocks (low P/E but the 'E' has to be positive, and/or low Debt/Equity).

1. Bring up Finviz.com.

2. Enter SPY (or any ETF that simulates the market).

3. If SMA-200% is negative, the market is not recovering, and you can skip the following steps.

4. Sell all contra ETFs and close all shorts if you have any.

5. Market recovery is confirmed when SMA-50% is more positive than SMA-200%. To illustrate this condition, SMA-200% is 2% and SMA-50% is 5%. Commit a large percent of cash (or all cash for aggressive investors) to stocks. If you do not know what to buy, buy SPY or an ETF that simulates the market.

Do the above once a month. When the SPY price is closer to SMA actions percentage, perform the above once a week. The charts and data for market timing described in this book are based on SMA-350 (Simple Moving Average) that is more preferable than this simple procedure, but it requires some simple charting.

Important Note

Predictions are predictions. However, the more educated that the guess is, the better chance the guess will materialize. It does not mean it will always materialize as the market changes and sometimes it is not rational.

Appendix 1 – All my books

- Complete the Art of Investing (highly recommended combining most of my books on investing). The Kindle version has over 850 pages (6*9), about 3 times the size of an investing book.
- Sector Rotation: 21 Strategies and another book Shorting (highly recommended for short-term investors) have more specific chapters on the topic and share many articles with "Complete the art of investing".
- Best stocks for 2022 (avail after Dec. 15, 2021).
- "Nuclear War with China".
- Books for today's market: Profit from Coming Market Crash.
- The following books are in a series: Finding Profitable Stocks, Market Timing and Scoring Stocks. Alternate books: Using Fidelity and Using Finviz.
- Books on strategies: "Profit from bull, bear and sideways markets" (Rotation + Momentum + ETF Rotation + trend following), Trading System (similar to printed version of Complete), Swing (Rotation +

Momentum), ETF Rotation for Couch Potatoes, Momentum, SuperStocks, Dividend, Penny & Micro Stock, and Retiree.
- Books for advance beginners: Be an expert (highly recommended), Introduce, Investing for Beginners, Beat Fund Managers, Profit via ETFs, Buffett, Ideas, Conservative and Top-Down.
- Miscellaneous: Lessons in Investing. Investing Strategies. Buy Low and Sell High. Buy High and sell Higher. Buffettology. Technical Analysis. Trading Stocks.
- Concise Editions and Introduction Editions are available at very low prices and are competitive with books of similar sizes (50 pages) and prices ($3 range).

Most books have paperbacks. Links and offers are subject to change without notice.

Best stocks to buy for 2022 (avail. after Dec. 15, 21)

We care about performance only. Not considering dividends and fees, my last three books in this series have beaten the SPY (the market to most) by **110%, 71% and 25%** from the publish date to 07/01/2021.

Book	Stocks	Return	Ann.	Beat SPY by
Best Book for 2021 2nd Edition	10	20%	52%	110%
Best Book for 2021	4	29%	52%	71%
Best Book to Buy from Aug, 2020	14	42%	45%	25%
Avg.	9	31%	50%	69%

Appendix 2 – Complete the Art of Investing

Instead of buying 16 books, why not buy one book (Complete the Art of Investing) consisting of 16 books? Besides saving money and your digital shelve space, it gives you quick reference and concentration on the topic you're currently interested in. It covers most investing topics in investing excluding speculative investing such as currency trading and day trading.
The Kindle version has about 850 pages (6*9), about the size of three books of average size. With the cost of $10 and at least 850 investing ideas, it is about one cent per idea. Most other books have only a few ideas in the entire book

The 16 books
This book "Complete Art of Investing" is divided into 16 books as follows. Click for the link to the book described in Amazon.com. I squeezed more than 3,000 pages into 850 pages by eliminating duplicated information such as evaluating stocks.

Book No.	Amazon.com
1	Simple techniques
2	Finding Stocks
3	Evaluating Stocks
4	Scoring Stocks
5	Trading Stocks
6	Market Timing
7	Strategies
8	Sector Rotation
9	Insider Trading
10	Penny Stocks & Micro Cap
11	Momentum Investing
12	Dividend Investing
13	Technical Analysis
14	Investing Ideas
15	The Economy
16	Buffettology

The book links are subject to change without notice.

"How to be a billionaire" is for beginners and couch potatoes, who can use the advanced features of this book in the simplest and less time-consuming techniques. Most advance users can skip this section unless they want to use some of the short cuts described.

We start with the basic books Finding Stocks, Evaluate Stocks, Trading Stocks and Market Timing. You can select and start with one of the many styles and strategies in investing such as swing trading and top-down strategy. Many tools are described in other books such as ETFs, technical analysis, covered calls and trading plan.

Many books start with "Why" to lure you to read more and are followed by "How" and then the theory behind the book.
If the book you're reading is beneficial to you, imagine how it would with 850 pages.

Most readers' comments are on "Debunk the Myths in Investing", which this book is originally based on. As of 2018, I did not know any of the commentators on my books.

"I skipped ahead to his chapter book 14 (of "Complete the Art of Investing"), Investment Advice just to get a feel of his writing style. His research is phenomenal and doesn't overwhelm with big words or catchy "sales-like" tactics.

I truly believe this ordinary man, Mr. Tony Pow, has a gift of explaining his experience as an investor without the bull crap of trying to make you buy his stuff. He seemingly just wants to share his knowledge, tips, and clarity of definitions for the kind of folks like me who want to understand something FIRST before jumping in with emotions of trying to make a boat load of money. I like the technical analysis side he brings.

Mr. Tony Pow talks about hidden gems in his book; well....quite frankly, he is a hidden gem. Thank you and I will also post my comments about this author to my Facebook page!" – JB on this book.

"Excellent book, recommend to all investors... great knowledge. It has fine-tuned my investing strategies... Your book is hard to set aside, as I read it all the time learning good techniques and analysis of stocks, ETF... Since I purchased your book in March, I have underlined, highlighted and placed tabs on top of pages for quick reference." – Aileron on this book.

"Tony, I just finished reading your 2nd edition. It's my pleasure to report that I found it most interesting. You're welcome to use this blurb if you like:

Debunk the Myths in Investing is an all-encompassing look at not only the most salient factors influencing markets and investors, but also a from-the-trenches look at many of the misconceptions and mistakes too many investors make. Reading this book may save not only time and aggravation but money as well!"

Joseph Shaefer, CEO, Stanford Wealth Management LLC.

"Tony, Great work!" from James and Chris, who are portfolio managers.

"'Debunk the Myths in Investing' is a comprehensive book on investing that deals with many aspects of this tense profession in which with a lot of knowledge and a bit of luck (or vice versa) one can greatly benefit...

Therefore 'Debunk the Myths in Investing' is an interesting book that on its 500 pages offer a lot of knowledge related to investing world and many practical advice, so I can recommend its reading if you're interested in this topic."
- Denis Vukosav, Top 500 Reviewers at Amazon.com.

"490 pages (Debunk) of a genius's ranting and hypothesis with various theories throughout, written light-heartedly with ample doses of humor...Yes, the myth of not being able to profitably time the market is BUSTED...

One might ask... Why is he giving away the results of his hard-earned research for only $20? He states that his children are not interested in investing and wants to share his efforts with the world." - Abe Agoda.

"Excellent book, recommend to all investors... great knowledge. It has fine-tuned my investing strategies... Your book is hard to set aside, as I read it all the time learning good techniques and analysis of stocks, ETF... Since I purchased your book in March, I have underlined, highlighted and placed tabs on top of pages for quick reference." - Aileron on this book.

"Great stuff, Tony. It's great to meet experienced traders such as yourself. I had a browse through the book and think your method is a little more refined than mine."
"Your strategy is very rules based and solid. I sometimes envy people who have developed something like this."

Making 50% in one month

I claim to have the best one-month performance ever for recommending 8 or more stocks without using options and leverage. My following return is 57% in a month or 621% annualized. They are slightly different as I calculated the average from the averages of three different accounts. The average buy date is 12/26/18 and the "current date" is 01/28/19.

The performance may not be repeated. I will use the same screen for the coming years and even the expected 10% (or 120% annualized) is very good.

I used the same screen for searching stock candidates. I spent a total of about 20 hours from Dec. 15, 2018 to Jan. 5, 2019.

Stock	Buy Price	Sold or Current Price	Buy date	Sold or Current date	Profit %	Profit % Ann.	Status
CHK	2.13	2.99	01/03/09	01/18/19	40%	982%	Sold
MNK	16.41	21.45	01/03/19	01/25/19	31%	510%	Sold
MNK	16.43	21.45	01/03/19	01/25/19	31%	507%	Sold
NNBR	5.68	8.58	12/26/18	01/28/19	51%	565%	
NNBR	5.72	8.58	12/26/18	01/28/19	66%	727%	
ESTE	4.35	6.45	12/26/18	01/18/19	48%	766%	Sold
LCI	4.61	8.29	12/21/18	01/28/19	80%	767%	
MDR	8.01	9.13	01/08/19	01/28/19	14%	255%	
YRCW	3.29	5.78	12/21/18	01/28/19	76%	727%	
YRCW	3.26	5.78	12/21/18	01/28/19	77%	742%	
ASRT	3.56	4.18	12/26/18	01/28/19	17%	193%	
UTCC	7.13	11.00	12/26/18	01/28/19	54%	600%	
YRCW	2.92	5.78	12/26/18	01/28/19	98%	1083%	

Best one-year return

I claim to have the best-performed article in Seeking Alpha history, an investing site, for recommending 15 or more stocks in one year after the publish date without using options and leverage.

https://seekingalpha.com/article/1095671-amazing-returns-velti-alcatel-lucent-alpha-natural-resources

Your choice

"Complete the art of investing" should be your first choice. If you are short-term trading, I recommend "Sector Rotation: 21 Strategies" and "Shorting Stocks /ETFs". These 3 books together with "Using Fidelity" share many articles.

My recommended stocks can be found in my "Best stocks" series. It would be published on Dec. 15 – it is not a promise. So far, this book and "Sector

Rotation: 21 Strategies" are my best sellers. All info are subject to change without notice.

Sector Rotation: 21 Strategies

In addition, as of 5/2020 I bet that no author besides me made **over 4 times** using sector rotation starting the amount more than his yearly salary then.

- On 5/26/2020, I searched for "Sector Rotation" under Amazon's Book. They are listed in the same order except my book Sector Rotation: 21 Strategies.

Book	Date	Size[1]	Kindle $[1]	Hard $
Sector Rotation: 21 Strategies	**05/2020**	**425**	**$9.95**	$24.95
Super Sectors	09/2010	289	$26.39	$49.95
Dual Momentum Investing	11/2014	240	$40.40	$42.20
Sector Investing	05/1996	260		$29.94
Sector Trading Strategies	08/2007	164	$26.39	$16.66
The Sector Strategist	03/2012	225	$26.39	$44.96
ETF Rotation	10/2012	125	**$9.95**	**$14.99**
Optimal... Sector Rotation	07/2015	80		$44.07

[1] From Amazon on size and prices as of 5/25/2020. Last update is 09/2021.

My book won in all categories except the price for hard copy in one. However, my book won as the lowest cost per page by a wide margin.

- I have **21** strategies in sector rotation while most books have only one. It ranges from simple rotation of a stock ETF and cash for beginners to many advanced strategies for experts. Most other books have one or two strategies.
- Andrew, a contributor on Sector Rotation article at Seeking Alpha, said, "Great stuff, Tony. It's great to meet experienced traders such as yourself. I had a browse through the book and think your method is a little more refined than mine."
- "You have written the book in a way that makes good and logical sense." Bill.
- Do not be fooled by past performances. Just check the recent performance of the top 50 stocks selected by IBD in the last five years. The mediocre result (hopefully it will change) could be due to too many followers and/or there is no evergreen strategy.
- I switched most (if not all) of my sector funds in April, 2000 from technology sectors to traditional sectors (better to money market fund). We can reduce losses by spotting market plunges and the sector trend.

Appendix 3 - Our window to the investing world

The paperback version of this chapter can be found in the following link.
http://ebmyth.blogspot.com/2013/11/web-sites.html

- **General**
  Wikipedia / Investopedia /Yahoo!Finance / MarketWatch / Cnnfn
  / Morningstar /CNBC / Bloomberg / WSJ / Barron's / Motley Fool /
  TheStreet

- **Evaluate stocks**
  Finviz / SeekingAlpha / MSN Money / Zacks / Daily Finance / ADR /
  Fidelity / Earnings Impact / OpenInsider / NYSE / NASDAQ / SEC /
  SEC for 10K and 10Q (quarterly) reports required to file for listed
  stocks in major exchanges.

- **Charts**
  BigCharts / FreeStockCharts / StockCharts /

- **Screens**
  Yahoo!Finance / Finviz / CNBC / Morningstar /

- **Besides stocks**
  123Jump / Hoover's Online / FINRA Bond Market Data / REIT /
  Commodity Futures / Option Industry

- **Vendors**
  AAII / Zacks / IBD / GuruFocus / VectorVest /
  Fidelity / Interactive Brokers / Merrill Lynch /

- **Economy.**
  Econday / EcoconStats / Federal Reserve / Economist /

- **Misc.**
  Dow Jones Indices / Russell / Wilshire /
  IRS / Wikinvest / ETF Database / ETF Trends /
  Nolo (estate planning) / AARP /

Appendix 4 - ETFs / Mutual Funds

What is an ETF

ETFs have basic differences from mutual funds: 1. Lower management expenses, 2. Trade ETFs same as stocks, and 3. Usually more diversified but not more selective than the related mutual funds such as NOBL vs FRDPX.

The major classifications of ETFs are 1. Simulating an index such as SPY, QQQ and DIA, 2. Simulating a sector such as XLE and SOXX, 3. Simulating an asset class such as GLD and SLV, 4. Simulating a country or a group of countries such as EWC and FXI, 5. Managed by a manager(s) such as ARKK, 6. Betting a market or sector to go down such as SH and PSQ, and 7. Leveraged (not recommended for beginners).

Fidelity: Index ETFs (https://www.fidelity.com/etfs/overview).

Wikipedia on ETF (http://en.wikipedia.org/wiki/Exchange-traded_fund).

List of ETFs
ETF database (Recommended): http://etfdb.com/
ETF Bloomberg: http://www.bloomberg.com/markets/etfs/
ETF Trends: http://www.etftrends.com/
A list of ETFs. Seeking Alpha.
http://etf.stock-encyclopedia.com/category/)
A list of contra ETFs (or bear ETFs)
http://www.tradermike.net/inverse-short-etfs-bearish-etf-funds/
Misc.: ETFGuide, ETFReplay
Fidelity low-cost index funds:
https://www.youtube.com/watch?v=zpKi4_lJvlY
Fidelity Annuity funds with performance data.
http://fundresearch.fidelity.com/annuities/category-performance-annual-total-returns-quarterly/FPRAI?refann=005

Other resources
Most subscription services offer research on ETFs. IBD has a strategy dedicated to ETFs and so does AAII to name a couple.

Seeking Alpha has extensive resources for ETF including an ETF screener and investing ideas. So is ETFdb.

Not all ETFs are created equal
Check their performances and their expenses.

When to use or not to use ETFs
I prefer sector mutual funds in some industries, as they have many bad stocks such as drug industry, banks, miners and insurers. Most mutual funds cannot time the market.

When you believe a sector is heading up (or contra ETF for heading down), but you do not have time to do research on specific stocks, buy an ETF for the sector; it is same for the market.

Half ETF
Taking out half of the stocks that score below the average in an index ETF could beat the same full ETF itself. I call it HETF (half the ETF). You heard it here first. To illustrate, sort the expected P/E (not including stocks with negative earnings) in ascending order and only include the stocks on the first half. Add more fundamental metrics. It will take a few minutes.

Disadvantages of ETFs
- When you have two stocks in a sector ETF one good one and one bad one, the ETF treats them the same. Stock pickers would buy the one that has a better appreciation potential.
- Sometimes the return could be misleading due to stock rotation. To illustrate this, on August 29, 2012, SHLD was replaced by LYB in a sector fund. SHLD was down by 4% and LYB was up by 4% primarily due to the switch. Unless you sell and buy at the right time (which is impossible), your return would not match the ETF's returns due to the replacement.
- Ensure the performance matches the corresponding index; it is hard due to excluding dividends.

Advantages of ETFs
- We have demonstrated that you can beat the market by using market timing. Between 2000 and Nov., 2013, you only exit and reenter the market 3 times and the result is astonishing.
- It is easy to rotate a sector vs. buying/selling all of the stocks in this sector. Rotating a sector is the same as trading a stock.
- The risk is spread out, and your portfolio is diversified especially for a market ETF or buying three or more ETFs in different sectors.
- Periodically the bad stocks in most funds are replaced by better stocks.
- Eliminate the time in researching stocks.

Leveraged ETFs

I do not recommend them. Some are 2x, 3x and even higher. They're too risky for beginners. However, when you are very sure or your tested strategy has very low drawdown, you may want to use them to improve performance. Most leveraged ETFs and contra ETFs have higher fees.

My basic ETF tables

I include some contra ETFs, mutual funds and Fidelity's annuity. Some of these may be interesting to you.

ETFs and funds come and go. Some ideas and classifications are my own interpretation. Refer to ETFdb for updated information. Not responsible for any error. Check out the ETF or fund before you take any action.

Table by market cap:

Category	ETF	Mutual Funds	Fidelity's Annuity	Contra ETF	Alternate
Size:					
Large Cap	DIA	See Blend		DOG	
	SPY			SH	FXAIX VOO
	QQQ			PSQ	FNCMX
	RYH				
Blend	IWD	BEQGX			
Growth	SPYG	FBGRX			FSPGX
Value	SPYV	DOGGX			FLCOX
Dividend	NOBL	FRDPX			
	VYM				
Mid Cap			FNBSC	MYY	
Blend	MDY	VSEQX			
Growth		STDIX			
		BPTRX			
Value		FSMVX			
Small Cap			FPRGC	SBB	FSSNX
Blend	IWM	HDPSX			
Growth		PRDSX			FECGX
Value		SKSEX			FISVX
Micro	IWC				
Multi					

Blend		VDEOX			
Growth		VHCOX			
Value		TCLCX			
Total					FSKAX
Bond					
Long Term (20)	VLV	BTTTX		TBF	
Mid Term (7 – 10)	VCIT	FSTGX			
Short Term (1 – 3 yrs.)	VCSH	THOPX			
Total	BOND	PONDX			
Corp Invest Grade	VCIT	NTHEX			
High Yield (junk)	PHB	SPHIX			
Muni	MUB	Check state			
Special situation					
Buy back	PKW				

Table by sectors:

Sector	ETF	Mutual Funds	Fidelity's Annuity
Banking[1]		FSRBK	
Regional	IAT		
Bio Tech	IBB	FBIOX	
	XBI	Large	
Consumer Dis.	XLY	FSCPX	FVHAC
Consumer Staple	XLP	FDFAX	FCSAC
Finance	KIE	FIDSX	FONNC
	IYF		
Energy	XLE	FSENX	FJLLC
Energy Service		FSESX	
Gold	GLD	FSAGX	
Gold Miner	GDX	VGPMX	
Health Care	IYH	FSPHX	FPDRC
	VHT	VGHCX	
House Builder	ITB	FSHOX	
	ITB	Perform	

Industrial	IYJ	FCYIX	FBALC
Material	VAW	FSDPX	
	IYM		
Oil	USO		
Oil Service	OIH	FSESX	
Oil Exploration	XOP		
Real Estate	VNQ	FRIFX	FFWLC
REIT	VNQ		
Retail	RTH	FSRPX	
	XRT		
Regional bank	KRE	FSRBX	
Semi Conduct	SMH		
Software	XSW	FSCSX	
	IGV		
Technology	XLK	FSPTX	FYENC
	FDN	FBSOX	
		ROGSX	
Telecomm.	VOX	FSTCX	FVTAC
Transport	XTN		
	IYT		
Utilities	XLU	FSUTX	FKMSC
Wireless		FWRLX	

Footnote. [1] Also check Finance.

Table by countries outside the USA:

Country	ETF	Mutual Funds	Fidelity's Annuity	Alternate
Australia	EWA			
Brazil	EWZ			
Canada	EWC	FICDX		
China	FXI	FHKCX		
EAFE	EFA			
Emerging	VWO	FEMEX	FEMAC	FPADX
Europe	VGK	FIEUX		
Global	KXI	PGVFX		
Greece	GREK			
India	INDY	MINDX		
Indonesia	EIDO			
Latin America	ILF	FLATX		
Nordic		FNORX		
Hong Kong	EWH			
Japan	EWJ	FJPNX		
S. Africa	EZA			
S. Korea	EWY	MAKOX		
Singapore	EWS			
Taiwan	EWT			
	TUR			
United Kingdom	EWU			
Foreign:				
Combination				
Intern. Div.	IDV			FTIHX
Small Cap	SCZ			
Value	EFV			
Europe	VGK			

#Filler: Honey, my book can play music.

https://www.youtube.com/watch?v=HxGT5z6d-GA&list=PLMZa6mP7jZ2b1otqG4tfbgZpLEdh6YiNF

It may cut down commercials by casting it to TV.